Staci LaToison

Money Moves

FROM **FINANCIAL** STRESS TO FINANCIAL **SUCCESS**

Money Moves

For more information, contact:
Fig Factor Media, LLC | www.figfactormedia.com
Her Money Moves |

Cover & Interior Layout Design: Marco Antonio Álvarez Rodríguez

Printed in the United States of America

ISBN: 978-1-961600-73-7

FIG FACTOR MEDIA

Money Moves

FROM **FINANCIAL** STRESS
TO FINANCIAL **SUCCESS**

Dedication

To my children, Sofia and DJ—You are my greatest motivation and my proudest joy. Everything I do, I do with your future in mind. Watching you grow reminds me daily why it's so important to lead with strength, love, and purpose.

To my parents, Sergio and June—Thank you for being my anchor, my example, and my support system. Your sacrifices, values, and belief in me have shaped the foundation I continue to build on. I carry your wisdom with me in every step I take.

To the women who are doing their best to hold it all together—especially the single mothers, the dreamers, the survivors, and the quiet warriors carrying the weight of financial stress in silence—this book is for you.

May you find in these pages not only guidance, but hope. May you remember that financial independence isn't a luxury—it's a lifeline. And no matter where you start, you have the power to change your story.

Acknowledgments

First and foremost, I want to thank my parents, Sergio and June, who always emphasized the importance of education. Your confidence in me gave me the foundation to dream bigger and expect more of myself. That foundation changed everything.

To my beloved abuela, Aida—your courage echoes through generations. At 19, you left Puerto Rico to clean houses in a country where you didn't speak the language. You worked tirelessly, sending money back to your family and ultimately bringing them to a better life. Your strength and sacrifice paved the way for all of us. You will always be my inspiration.

To Sofia and DJ, my beautiful children—you are my why. Your love, your laughter, and your belief in me keep me going every day. Thank you for your unconditional love and for being my reason and my reward.

To my nieces and nephews, who bring me joy and light—you remind me why it matters to lead by example. I hope the paths I've walked inspire you to forge even bigger ones.

To the guests of the *Her Money Moves* podcast—you've each inspired me in profound ways. Your vulnerability, brilliance, and stories have shaped this book as much as my own experiences. I grow with every conversation, and I'm honored to amplify your voices.

To the *Her Money Moves* community—my "Money Movers"—thank you for showing up with curiosity and courage. You are proof that women are ready to change the narrative around money. I'm here for all of it—every win, every breakthrough, every aha moment.

To my dream team—thank you for believing in our mission and helping bring it to life. Your support means more than I can say.

To my closest friends and cousins who've stood by me through every high and low—thank you for being my sounding board, my cheerleaders, and my reality check when I needed it most.

And finally, to Deborah LeBlanc—your story changed mine. When I became a young mother at 17 and thought my dreams were over, your example reminded me that they weren't. You showed me what was possible. You were living proof that resilience wasn't just a word—it was a path forward. Thank you for being that light when I needed it most.

This book is a love letter to resilience. And to every woman who's ever wondered if she could do it—I'm here to tell you: *you can.*

Contents

Contents

Chapter 1

Breaking the Silence

The Money Conversation

"We don't grow up talking about money, yet we make financial decisions every single day."
~Staci LaToison

Money is a thread that runs through every part of life. It influences where we live, how we raise our families, the opportunities we pursue, and the choices we make every single day. And yet, money remains one of the hardest things to talk about. Not because it's irrelevant—but because it's deeply personal, often emotional, and for many, shaped by silence, fear or unspoken struggles.

For most people, the silence around money starts at home. Financial matters are rarely part of everyday conversation. Then comes school, where students are required to master algebra and calculus but rarely taught how to build a budget, evaluate a loan, or understand a credit score. And by the time young adults are out on their own, the pressure is on to "figure it out" without the tools or confidence to make informed financial decisions.

Credit card companies line up at college campuses, handing out high-interest credit with no questions asked—no job required, no understanding necessary. The consequences of those early decisions often take years to undo. And throughout it all, the silence persists.

WHY MONEY FEELS SO COMPLICATED

Have you ever felt like money conversations weren't meant for you? Truthfully, sometimes it feels like the financial world is speaking a language designed to confuse you. You turn on CNBC or Bloomberg, and it's all green and red charts, acronyms, and jargon that makes you want to shut it off.

You're not alone—this is where we rewrite the story together. The system wasn't built to include everyone. But that doesn't mean we wait for permission to join the conversation. Financial knowledge isn't reserved for the elite. You deserve to understand your money, speak the language, and make informed decisions that grow it exponentially with confidence. Let's break it down, make it human, and help you step fully into your financial power.

First, let's talk about why money, of all things, has become such a taboo topic.

Historically, the discomfort in talking about finances is rooted in societal structures. Cultural norms have long suggested that talking about money is inappropriate—especially when it comes to income, debt, or financial struggles. This silence often allows financial inequality to persist unchecked and discourages people from advocating for themselves or seeking transparency around salaries, investments, and other opportunities.

At work, this reluctance to talk about salaries can show up as uncertainty when negotiating a raise. In relationships, it can manifest as conflict, confusion, or avoidance. And on a personal level, the silence can foster anxiety, guilt, and a lack of clarity around values and goals.

But here's the truth: the more people talk about money—honestly, openly, and without shame—the more empowered we become.

Financial confidence comes from education and awareness. Transparency leads to better decisions. And meaningful conversations can shift everything—from your mindset to your legacy.

There's strength in starting exactly where you are. Whether you're fresh out of school or decades into your career, it's never too late to take control and move forward. The silence around money doesn't serve anyone. Breaking it might just change your life for the better.

REFLECTION QUESTIONS:

- *What's the first memory you have about money? How did it make you feel—safe, anxious, confused or empowered?*
- *Whose voice shaped your earliest money beliefs? Are those beliefs still serving you today?*

Chapter 2

Money Mindset

Understanding Your Financial DNA

"Your childhood experiences shape your financial future more than you realize."
~Staci LaToison

Everyone carries a unique financial blueprint—an internal map formed by family dynamics, cultural expectations, and life experiences. This "financial DNA" quietly shapes how we save, spend, give, and plan for the future. In fact, most of us are following a script we didn't even realize we inherited.

Maybe you grew up watching a parent stretch every dollar, or perhaps witnessed financial hardships that felt constant and inescapable. Some of us grew up determined to never repeat those struggles. Others internalized beliefs like money is always scarce, always stressful, always out of reach. Over time, those beliefs become the lens through which every financial decision is made.

However, it's not just our upbringing. The broader culture plays a role, too. We live in a society that rewards overconsumption and equates success with spending. Messages are everywhere: new car, designer clothes, bigger house, buy now, worry later. Meanwhile, conversations around budgeting, saving, or building wealth are often missing or misunderstood as something "only for the wealthy."

Understanding your financial DNA means taking a step back and asking: *Where did these beliefs come from?* Maybe it was growing up in a home where financial silence was the norm, with a parent who managed everything without sharing the "how." Or maybe it's rooted in financial trauma—a job loss, a divorce, or a sudden crisis that shook your sense of security.

Financial independence isn't just about dollars—it's about choices. It means having the freedom to leave toxic situations, both personal and professional. It's the ability to be self-sufficient and care for loved ones while building a life rooted in your values, not fear. When you start to shift your financial mindset, money becomes a tool, not a stressor. It can help you reclaim your time, protect your peace, and unlock new possibilities.

That shift takes work. It might mean cutting

unnecessary expenses. Confidently advocating for that raise. Investing in yourself. Talking to a financial advisor (yes, even if you don't feel "rich enough"). Because when you know better, you can do better—and it all starts with curiosity, honesty, and the decision to take control of your financial story.

Here's the good news: financial mindsets aren't fixed. Your financial DNA may have been inherited, but it doesn't have to be permanent. With intention, education, and practice, you can evolve it into something stronger, healthier, and fully aligned with who you are now and who you're becoming.

REFLECTION QUESTIONS:

- *Which inherited money beliefs are you ready to rewrite starting today?*
- *What would change in your life if you fully owned your financial power—personally, professionally, generationally?*
- *What's one step I can take this week to align my mindset with the future I want?*

Chapter 3

The Why Factor

Making Purpose-Driven Money Moves

"At 25, I stopped renting someone else's dream and bought my son a backyard full of dreams. That was my why."

~Staci LaToison

Everyone has a "why"—a reason to save, to plan, to do the hard things now for something better tomorrow. Whether it's building generational wealth, retiring with peace of mind, owning a home, or making sure their kids are better off than they were. Whatever it is, your "why" matters—because without it, money tends to disappear as fast as it appears.

We live in a treat yourself and YOLO culture. Delayed gratification isn't trending—but financial peace never goes out of style. With one click, anything can show up on your doorstep—shoes, meal kits, or Amazon 'necessities' you forgot you ordered. But just because you can buy something doesn't mean you *should*. That's where your why becomes powerful. It gives spending a purpose—and saving a reward.

The truth is, financial security doesn't happen by accident—it's a money move. It takes intention. That means thinking ahead, asking hard questions, and saying no to short term temptations so you can say yes to long-term freedom.

I get it. Buying a home at 25 wasn't easy. It meant skipping dinners out, passing on impulse buys, and spontaneous fun. But every time I watched my son cannonball into the backyard pool with his cousins and friends—I remembered exactly why I made those sacrifices. That sense of pride didn't come from the house itself—it came from the money moves I made to build it.

Let's be clear, a high income doesn't equal wealth. You can earn six figures and still live paycheck to paycheck. Wealth is about what you build, not just what you earn. It starts with clarity, discipline, and the courage to make smart money moves that align with your dreams.

Paying rent may give you a roof over your head, but it's also putting money into someone else's pocket. When you invest in assets like real estate, a business, or retirement accounts, you start putting that money to work for you. Ask yourself: Are my dollars building equity or just disappearing? True wealth isn't about fancy things—it's about peace of mind, ownership, and the power to build a life on your terms.

That's what money moves are all about. They're not always flashy, but they're always intentional. They're the quiet sacrifices that turn into loud victories.

None of this is about perfection. Some people save consistently. Others start late. Most of us fall somewhere in between. But no matter where you are today, you can always pivot. You can reset and take one bold step toward the future you deserve. It starts with asking yourself: *What is my why?*

So, start with your why. Then look at your habits. Trim the extras—cancel a subscription, brew your own coffee, cook instead of ordering out. Or go bigger—setup an auto transfer to savings, open that investment account and meet with a financial advisor. Every step counts.

Because one day, future you is going to thank you for making smart, intentional money moves now.

REFLECTION QUESTIONS:

- *What is your "why" for building wealth? How does it influence your financial decisions today?*
- *What's one money move you can make this week that brings you closer to financial freedom?*
- *Where are your dollars going—toward your goals, or toward distractions?*

Chapter 4

Set It, Don't Forget It

Making Your Financial Goals Real

"You can't manifest millions without a roadmap and a mindset to match."
~Staci LaToison

When it comes to money, hoping for the best isn't a strategy. It's a gamble. And yet, too many people go through life with vague financial dreams. One day, I'll own a home. One day, I'll start saving. One day, I'll retire comfortably.

The reality is, "one day" won't come without a plan. Goals turn dreams into decisions, not wishful thinking. But real, written, specific, and bold goals—backed by timelines and steps that actually move the needle—do. Because you can't hit a target you haven't defined.

Financial goals aren't just about numbers—they're deeply connected to your why. Want to buy a home in three years? That's not just about mortgage rates—it's about freedom, stability, wealth-building, and maybe giving your kids a backyard where they can laugh, run, and dream big.

Saving for retirement? That's about peace of mind and knowing you'll have options—and won't have to become a financial burden relying on others later in life. Retirement shouldn't feel like a cliff—it should feel like a runway. And that future starts with the money moves you make today.

The first step is clarity. Start simple. Write it down. On paper, in an app, or pinned to your vision board, make your goals visible and specific. Next, map out the path. If it's saving for a down payment, figure out how much you need and what you can set aside each month. Tackling debt? List your balances, interest rates, and a timeline for knocking them out. Dreaming of launching your own business? Start by setting a budget and getting crystal clear on what that leap will really require—mentally, financially, and emotionally. (And trust me, I've got a whole other book on the way that dives deep into this journey.)

And let's be honest—sometimes those numbers will slap you with truth. Maybe you're spending more than you earn. Maybe it's time to advocate for a raise, pick up a side hustle, or finally cancel that subscription your forgot about six months ago. This isn't failure, it's feedback. Data is power.

GET EVERYONE ON THE SAME PAGE

If you're in a relationship, a financial "check-in" is a must. Real alignment means shared vision and shared responsibility. Money fights often come from miscommunication and misalignment.

Goals need maintenance. Just like your car needs tune-ups, your financial plan does too. Schedule monthly check-ins with yourself or your household. Ask: What are your priorities? What's working? What's not? Are we still on track—or did Amazon, Uber Eats, and life throw us off? It's about awareness, accountability, and giving yourself permission to pivot when needed.

And while you're at it, don't forget to build in a cushion. An emergency fund—ideally three months of living expenses—can be the difference between a detour and a full-on derailment. Because chaos doesn't send calendar invites in advance.

The car will break down. Pipes will burst. Roofs will leak. Storms will hit when you least expect them. A medical emergency, whether it's you, your family, or your fur baby, can throw everything off track.

And unfortunately, in today's economy layoffs are becoming more common. Your job could disappear with zero warning. A cushion won't stop life from swinging, but it gives you the gloves to fight back.

Remember, when you've set goals, stayed flexible, and built in a cushion, those disruptions won't be disasters. They'll become speed bumps. And you, my friend, already know how to navigate them and keep driving forward.

REFLECTION QUESTIONS:

- *What are three financial goals that light you up—and why do they matter to you?*
- *What's one money move I can adjust right now to better meet my goals?*

6816 L

Chapter 5

Picture Your Prosperity

What does wealth mean to you?

"Wealth is the freedom to live life on your terms—and the confidence to know you'll be okay no matter what."
~Staci LaToison

When you hear the word wealth, what's the first image that pops into your mind? A vacation on the Amalfi Coast? A paid-off mortgage? Maybe it's something more subtle—like checking your bank app and feeling peace instead of panic.

Whatever it looks like, here's the truth—wealth isn't one-size-fits-all. Prosperity is personal. And your vision of financial success doesn't have to look like anyone else's. It is yours to define—and yours to claim.

For some, it's about freedom—saying "yes" to opportunities without money being the dealbreaker. It's planning an epic family vacation and making unforgettable cherished memories. It's living by the water because it lights up your soul. For others, it's knowing your savings account has your back. That your child can go to college debt free. Or confidently knowing you'll never again have to choose between paying rent or buying groceries.

There was a time in my life when abundance meant the budget was wide open—and so was the joy. I had the nanny, the housekeeper, the driver, lavish vacations around the globe, the freedom to say yes without a second thought. And honestly, it felt amazing. I had the time of my life! But back then, I wasn't making intentional money moves. I wasn't thinking long term. I wasn't building legacy. Hindsight? It's always 20/20. I was young, in my 20s, and just living in the moment.

Looking back, I realize that with more intention, I could've used that abundance to invest in real estate, tech, or businesses that build generational wealth. That's why I'm sharing this with you now—so you don't just spend money. You move it with purpose.

Here's something worth noting, prosperity isn't just about what you can buy—it's about how you feel. Do you feel safe? Empowered? Energized by your future? Or are you constantly stressed, stretching every dollar, surviving instead of thriving?

Real wealth is peace of mind. It's finally

paying off that lingering credit card debt. It's being able to say yes to your child's summer camp. It's saying yes to working in a career that you love—not one that just pays the bills. It's living in alignment with your values—not your fears. It's freedom of health, freedom of peace, and freedom of time. That's the kind of abundance that makes every money move matter.

MAKE THE VISION REAL

What does your version of wealth look like? Not your neighbor's. Not an influencer's. Yours. Is it a fully funded retirement? A multi-unit investment property? Or finally starting that business that you've been dreaming about for years?

Grab a journal or vision board and get specific. What are you doing in your wealthy life? Who's with you? How does it feel to lead decisions with power, not panic? Once you have the vision, list the first three money moves to get closer. Then, take action. Make progress. Rinse and repeat until your reality matches your dream.

It's all about your prosperity and your pace. Here's the most powerful truth: you don't have to wait to feel prosperous. Every small decision you make today—setting a budget, skipping the impulse buy, investing in yourself—builds the foundation for the life you're meant to live.

Be patient with the process. Stay committed to your vision. And know this: every intentional money move you make today is writing the legacy you'll live tomorrow.

REFLECTION QUESTIONS:

- *When I envision financial success, what does it include—and how does it feel?*
- *What's one money move I can make this week to bring that vision of wealth to life?*

Debit

Chapter 6

Help! I'm Drowning!

Credit & Debt – Rewriting Your Relationship with Borrowed Money

"Life is unpredictable. Your finances shouldn't be."
~Staci LaToison

Credit is a tool, not a trap. But you have to know how to use it. Credit can open doors—to homes, businesses, education and opportunities to build wealth. But for many, debt can feel like quicksand. One minute you're fine but one missed payment can snowball and suddenly you're gasping for air with a mountain of debt and stress heavy on your heart. And when you're just trying to make ends meet, the system can feel rigged against you. The worst part? That pit-in-your-stomach feeling that it'll never get better.

But it can. And it starts with honesty.

Debt doesn't show up overnight. It creeps in—through unexpected car repairs, medical bills, job loss, or even a few too many swipe-and-go moments. Suddenly, you're looking at balances you can't believe. You're wondering how you got here, and more importantly, how to get out.

Step One: Face It to Fix It.

Avoidance is expensive. The first step to reclaiming your financial power? Face it—fearlessly. Write it all down. Every credit card. Every loan. The balances, interest rates, and minimum payments. Whether you use an app, a spreadsheet, or a crumpled notepad from your junk drawer—just get it out of your head and onto the page. When you see the full picture, you can finally start painting a new one.

Step Two: Choose Your Plan of Attack.

On-time payments are the single biggest factor in your credit score. Even if it's the minimum—pay it. Want a quick win? Start with the smallest balances and knock them out (hello, momentum!). Want to save the most long-term? Hit those high-interest accounts first to stop the financial bleeding. Either way, progress is power. Credit utilization (how much of your available credit you're using) affects your score. Keeping usage under 30% is ideal.

Step Three: Take a Deep Breath—and Call Your Creditors.

Let them know you're navigating a financial hardship. Some may offer lower rates, payment plans, or even forgiveness options. Some won't. But here's the truth—*silence will never save you money.* Action might.

Here's a common mistake to avoid—don't rush to close your accounts. Even if you cut up the cards, keeping the lines open helps maintain your credit history. This plays a major role in your score. Let your discipline—not a closure—do the work.

A reality check for you: add up the interest you're paying each month. That number might blow your mind. It might even make you furious, because that's money you're giving away. That's future-you's vacation, home renovation, or emergency cushion—gone. Instead, it's going to the banks.

Let that fire fuel your comeback. Because once you face the numbers, you can finally start flipping them. Debt is a cycle, and it's one you can break. It takes self-discipline and it takes time. But the freedom on the other side is worth it.

Being poor is expensive. The lower your credit score, the more you'll pay in interest. If your score is low, you're seen as a higher risk—which means higher rates on everything from credit cards to car loans to insurance. You could end up paying thousands more over time for the exact same thing someone with good credit gets at a fraction of the cost. Meanwhile, high income earners leverage tax strategies and investment loopholes to reduce their tax bills, sometimes paying less in taxes than those in lower income tax brackets. The system wasn't built with fairness in mind. But understanding it gives you the power to navigate it differently.

This is why it's not just about paying debt—it's about building financial knowledge and systems that protect you. You don't want to be cash-poor, asset-poor, and constantly playing catch-up. You want financial flexibility, so when life happens, you have room to breathe.

If you're feeling overwhelmed—breathe. You're not alone. There's a world of support at your fingertips—books and courses like "Money Moves," podcasts like *Her Money Moves,* apps, and trusted financial planners ready to walk the journey with you.

What's stopping you from reaching out to a mentor or coach who's already walked the path you're on? Sometimes, the breakthrough comes from a single conversation, a single step.

You don't have to have it all figured out—you just need to start. Start messy. Start unsure.

Just remember, shame has no seat at this table—only strategy, strength, and next steps. It's about drawing a line in the sand and declaring, "I'm done feeling buried. I'm ready to breathe, rise, and reclaim my power." Because the truth is, you don't need all the answers to begin—just courage to take the first step. And if you're reading this, you already are.

REFLECTION QUESTIONS:

- *What's one step I can take today to face my debt head-on?*
- *How can I shift from feeling stuck to feeling financially empowered?*

Chapter 7

Million-Dollar Mindset, Million-Dollar Moves

Champagne Wishes or Compound Interest?

"A million dollars doesn't go as far as you think."
~Staci LaToison

Ever daydream about what you'd do if a million dollars landed in your lap? Is that dream to pay off debt? Buy your dream home? Take that dream trip? You're not alone. But here's the truth—a million dollars isn't what it used to be, and without a plan, it can vanish faster than you think.

This chapter is your invitation to make Million-Dollar Money Moves—on purpose, with purpose. Because it's not about luck, it's about readiness.

Start by asking yourself, "Where would it go? Would I invest it? Pay off my mortgage? Fund a business?" Here's the reality check: a million dollars doesn't guarantee freedom. Between inflation, taxes, healthcare, and everyday life, that money can slip through your fingers faster than you think. Without a strategy, a dream windfall can become a financial disaster.

It's why so many lottery winners, pro athletes, celebrities, and influencers go from millions to zero—fast. Because when you don't have a plan, it doesn't matter how much you earn. Wealth without wisdom is a setup for loss. But here's the good news: every decision you make with that money is a seed. Plant it with intention, and it can grow into real security—not just a temporary shopping spree.

What would a smart, future-focused money mover do? You diversify. You protect. You grow. You:

- Invest a portion in stocks—even if it makes you a little nervous.
- Pay down high-interest debt (because it's stealing your wealth).
- Buy real estate or consider income-producing property.
- Invest in yourself through business or education.
- Don't forget: a life insurance policy that builds cash value is a long-term power move.

And don't sleep on the power of compound interest, as Warren Buffett has demonstrated. Even small, consistent investments can transform into long-term income if you give them time. That's how you turn a moment of abundance into a lifetime of wealth.

Either way, the goal stays the same: make your money work harder than you do.
Think about what matters—retirement peace of mind, your child's future, the freedom to choose what's next on your terms. Because having money isn't enough—knowing how to manage it is the ultimate power move.

So, whether you're dreaming of that million, building toward it, or already there—get ready. Talk to a financial advisor. Map out your goals. Understand your tax landscape. And most importantly, stay rooted in intention.

Being a millionaire isn't a finish line—it's a launchpad. Whether you earn it, inherit it, or build it from the ground up, your next move matters. Don't just dream of having more—decide how you'll manage it when it comes. That's the real difference between a temporary win and lasting wealth.

This chapter isn't about fantasy or winning the lottery—it's about financial readiness. Because when your moment comes, I want you to meet it with confidence. That's a true Money Move.

REFLECTION QUESTIONS:

- *If a million dollars landed in your account today, what would your first three Money Moves be—and why?*
- *What steps would you take to make sure the money lasts?*

Chapter 8

The Currency of Connection

Who You Know Fuels Your Growth

"IYKYK. Build circles that challenge you, grow with you, and open doors you didn't even know existed."

~Staci LaToison

You can't close a gap if you don't know it exists.

Most of us weren't handed financial blueprints growing up. We learned algebra but not how to budget. We memorized historical dates but not how to manage debt. Meanwhile, people with access to financial education and well-connected networks have been stacking wins for generations. It's not just luck—it's legacy.

That's why financial literacy matters—it's your power play. It's the difference between living paycheck to paycheck and building a lasting future. Knowing how to protect your peace, grow your income, invest in your future, and make confident decisions isn't a luxury—it's an essential money move.

Here's the twist: knowledge alone isn't enough. You also need access. You need people. A network of mentors, advisors, and champions who help you turn your goals into a plan.

If you're the smartest—or wealthiest—person in your circle, it's time to find a new room.

I once heard Alex Rodriguez say he leveled up because Warren Buffett and Magic Johnson are his mentors. That's not coincidence—that's intentional proximity. While most of us don't have access to billionaires on speed dial, we do have access to someone in our community, network, or industry who is one step ahead and willing to share the roadmap.

So, start where you are. Ask questions. Reach out. Your next mentor might be a local business owner, a LinkedIn connection, or someone you've admired from afar. Trust me—people love to pour into those who are ready to receive.

When selecting a financial advisor, remember that you have the upperhand. Professionals want your business, and you get to choose your dream team.

Own Your Power. Build Your Circle. Make Your Move.

Your wealth circle doesn't have to be big—it needs to be strategic:

- A financial planner who listens and empowers you.
- A tax expert who knows how to maximize what you earn.
- A lawyer who helps protect your assets and legacy.
- An investment group, like angel investors where you can review investment opportunities, apply due diligence, and bounce ideas and questions off of.
- A coach or accountability partner who challenges your growth.

These are your power players.

The people who help close the gap between where you are and where you're going. Wealth isn't just about what you earn—it's about what you know, who you trust, and how you move.

And when you combine information with intention? You become unstoppable.

REFLECTION QUESTIONS:

- *Who is currently in my financial inner circle—and who's missing?*
- *Where can I expand my access to trusted expert advice and mentorship?*
- *What's one step I can take this week to invest in my financial network?*

BIZ Company
14 Main Street, PA
Tel. (011) 527-2960
DATE
PAY TO THE ORDER OF
One Million Dollars 00/100
$ 1.000.000.00
Autorized Signature
Saving Bank
271 Stars Avenue, George Town
Tel. (001) 819-0672
BANK
79 81320 76145 10659

Chapter 9

More than a Paycheck

Building Passive and Multiple Income Streams

"Your salary is a starting point—not a safety net. Build wealth in your sleep."
~Staci LaToison

Your 9-to-5 was never designed to fund your dreams. If we've learned anything over the last few years, it's that job security is fragile. Layoffs, reorganizations, AI disruption—they can all shift your world overnight. Depending on one income stream in today's economy is risky and outdated.

This reality makes building multiple income streams essential for financial resilience in our rapidly changing economy. The goal isn't working yourself into exhaustion but creating layers of security that provide both protection and possibility.

When money flows in from multiple directions, you gain something invaluable—choice. You're no longer trapped by financial necessity or forced to tolerate toxic work environments simply to survive. Multiple income streams create breathing room, allowing decisions based on values rather than desperation.

MAKE MONEY MOVE—FROM ONE STREAM TO MANY

Your path to income diversification starts with what's already in your hands:

- Got a skill? Monetize it.
- Got a story? Sell it.
- Got knowledge? Teach it.
- Got access? Leverage it.

You don't need to launch an empire overnight. Maybe you tutor. DJ weddings. Consult. Write grants. Referee. Rent out a space. Host an online class. Every drop adds to the stream.

FROM SIDE HUSTLE TO PASSIVE POWER

Passive income is the real flex: money that flows even when you're on vacation, asleep, or living your life.

These side pursuits don't have to become full-blown businesses overnight. They just need to bring in consistent income—streams that add up over time and give you more freedom, stability, and choice.

TOP INCOME STREAMS EVERY MONEY MOVER SHOULD KNOW

Earned Income: Your paycheck—your starting point, not your end game. Whatever you do, take advantage of that 401k match! That's free money to multiply your wealth.

Investments: Build wealth while you sleep. Stocks, ETFs, index funds, and dividend portfolios that grow over time and work harder than you do.

Real Estate & Rentals: Monthly cash flow, long-term equity, and tax advantages. Whether it's long-term rentals, short-term rentals like Airbnb or VRBO, multi-family units, storage units, purchasing acres of land, or REITs—real estate is a legacy move.

Angel Investing & Venture Capital: These might sound exclusive, but they're becoming more accessible ways to build long term, passive wealth. While riskier than traditional income streams, they offer the potential for significant returns—and the chance to support innovative founders and companies you believe in. Whether through direct investments or venture funds, this path is about planting financial seeds that can grow quietly behind the scenes. Just remember, it's a long game, a marathon, not a race. You won't see a return for nearly a decade, so be ready to part with the money with that realization in mind.

Side Hustles: Use what you've got. Freelance, consult, cater, coach, tutor—turn your skills into extra income.

Digital Products & Platforms: Courses, templates, ebooks, paid communities, and content platforms like YouTube or Substack. Create once, earn repeatedly.

Franchises: Buy into an established brand with built-in systems and support. A smart way to scale without starting from scratch.

Revenue-Generating Businesses: start small with vending machines, photo booths, laundromats, or event rentals. These lowtouch models can bring in cash on autopilot. You could purchase a revenue generating professional service business such as Accounting and Tax firms, Insurance, HVAC, Roofing, Electricians, Landscaping, etc. They are ready to retire and their kids don't want to take over the business, but you could.

Remember that financial diversification provides more than economic security—it delivers peace of mind. When unexpected expenses arise or opportunities emerge, you'll face them with confidence rather than panic.

Your salary was never meant to carry all your dreams. Diversify your income, and you diversify your freedom.

REFLECTION QUESTIONS:

- *What income-generating skill, interest, or asset do I already have that I haven't leveraged yet?*
- *What small, strategic move can I make this week to start building an additional income stream?*

Chapter 10

The Financial Roadmap

From Wandering to Wealth-building

"Wealth starts with a strategy."
~Staci LaToison

Reality is, the path to financial freedom doesn't just happen—it's built intentionally, one bold money move at a time.

Between rising living costs, credit card debt, student loans, rent or mortgage, and trying to plan for retirement, it's easy to feel like you're juggling chaos. But if you're winging it financially, you're not building—you're wandering.

That's why a financial roadmap is a necessity.

Think of it like Waze for your money. It helps you see where you are, where you're going, and what detours to avoid. And if you're serious about leveling up, partnering with a financial planner can be a game-changer.

Don't wait until you "have more money" to create a roadmap. A great financial planner looks at the whole picture—your income, assets, debt, and goals—and helps you chart a course tailored to you.

You don't need to be rich to work with a financial advisor. That's one of the biggest myths out there. Many planners work on a percentage basis, meaning they grow when you grow. The earlier you begin, the more powerful the compounding effect becomes—not just on your money, but on your confidence.

Yes, it takes courage to open your financial books. You might not feel proud of your finances right now. Maybe you're carrying debt, or your budget feels out of control. But that's exactly when it helps to seek a lifeline.

A planner isn't there to judge—trust me, they've seen it all. Their job is to support you, guide you, and give your goals a clear timeline, target, and track to follow. That's a true game-changer.

Working with a planner also brings accountability. It's one thing to tell yourself you'll save more or invest next year. It's another to have someone checking in with you, showing you progress, and adjusting your plan when life shifts—which it always does.

Think of it like a GPS. You might still hit traffic or detours, but the route is always recalculating, keeping you headed toward your destination.

Having a roadmap leads to better protection, starting with lining up a cash cushion before you need it. Set a minimum savings goal—ideally two to three months of fixed costs so you're not one emergency away from a crisis. As the saying goes, "Cash is like oxygen—it's always better to raise it when you don't need it."

And if you're in a relationship, don't skip the money talks. Financial alignment is just as important as emotional alignment. Sit down. Share your numbers. Map your goals. Celebrate your wins. A shared financial vision isn't just smart—it's a form of intimacy. When you and your partner are aligned on money goals, values, and habits, you're not just building wealth—you're building trust, teamwork, and a future you both believe in.

But what if your visions don't align? To me, it's not just a red flag—it's a deal breaker. Your financial roadmap can reveal whether you're truly on the same path or headed in opposite directions. Either way, that insight is powerful—and it gives you the clarity to move forward with intention and save headaches and heartbreak in the future.

Make money moves with purpose. Your future isn't a guess—it's a series of bold, intentional moves starting now.

REFLECTION QUESTIONS:

- *I have a clear roadmap for my money, or am I just coasting?*
- *What's one Money Move I can make this week to shift from uncertainty to clarity?*
- *Who can I trust to help me get there faster and smarter?*

Chapter 11

Cutting Through the Noise

Simplify. Prioritize. Thrive

"Financial freedom begins the moment you stop financing distractions and start funding your future."
~Staci LaToison

We live in a world of excess. Too many subscriptions. Too many temptations. Too many reasons to spend before we even think. From one-click checkouts to flash-sale countdowns, modern money culture is engineered to keep you on autopilot—and off balance.

Financial freedom isn't just about making more money—it's about managing it with intention. Less spending. Less clutter. Less distraction. The real magic happens when you quiet the noise and tune into what truly matters.

THE FIRST STEP: AUDIT THE EXTRAS

Start by taking inventory. Download your bank and credit card statements. Highlight every automatic payment. Circle the things you forgot you even signed up for. Ask yourself:

- How many subscriptions are you paying for and not using?
- How often are you ordering takeout when there's perfectly good food at home?
- How many "just this once" purchases are showing up... again and again?

Because that $14.99 here and $7.99 there? It's not harmless—*it's leaking possibility*. That's not just money—it's momentum. It could be building your emergency fund. Funding your first investment account. Paying for a business course, a weekend getaway, or your child's extracurriculars.

This is how you take your money off autopilot—and start making intentional moves that build your future.

THE NEXT MOVE: ALIGN YOUR SPENDING WITH YOUR POWER

Every dollar you earn is a decision. Are you giving your money direction—or letting it drift?

Try this: Match each major expense to a personal value. If it doesn't support your goals, it's noise. When your money moves are rooted in clarity, you don't just save—you amplify.

MAKE SAVING FEEL LIKE WINNING

Financial discipline doesn't have to feel like punishment. Make it playful:

- Brew your coffee instead of buying it—transfer the $8 into a "money moves" account.
- Cook at home four nights a week—pay off a credit card with the difference.
- Track the small wins. Celebrate progress. Compete with yourself.

Gamify your goals and give your discipline a dopamine boost.

MINDSET IS THE TRUE MULTIPLIER

Your mindset moves your money more than any budget ever will. Emotional spending—whether triggered from boredom, stress, or even celebration can quietly drain your momentum and pull you off course. But when you shift your money mindset, everything changes.

Before your next swipe, pause and ask: Is this a reward—or a reaction? What you eliminate today could become the fuel for your next bold move tomorrow.

When your spending aligns with your priorities, your money doesn't just grow—it gains power. You feel lighter. More in control. More unstoppable.

REFLECTION QUESTIONS:

- *What am I currently paying for that no longer aligns with my values or vision?*
- *If I eliminated 3 financial distractions, how would I reinvest that energy—or that money—into my goals?*

Chapter 12

Rethinking Retirement

Reality Check and Redefined Freedom

"Retirement today looks nothing like our parents' retirement."
~Staci LaToison

For decades, retirement was sold as the ultimate reward for loyalty and longevity. You'd work at one company, collect your pension, kick back, and enjoy the fruits of your labor. But that model has expired. The world has changed, and so has what it takes to retire well.

We're living longer, navigating more expensive healthcare, supporting multigenerational families, and redefining success on our own terms. Retirement isn't vanishing—it's evolving. The rules are changing, and it's time to adapt.

Let's bust a few myths.

Myth #1: *You'll spend less in retirement.*

Maybe—but not likely. Sure, you might save on commuting or office lunches, but other expenses creep in fast. Healthcare costs increase. Home repairs don't stop. You finally have time to travel more but travel expenses can take a toll. And if you haven't paid off your mortgage or you're still helping adult children or grandchildren, your monthly outflow might look a lot like it does today. Retirement doesn't mean life slows down—it means your money moves differently.

Myth #2: *Social Security will cover your needs.*

Spoiler alert: it won't. Social Security is a supplement, not a strategy. It barely covers the basics and for younger generations, its future is uncertain.

Myth #3: *Once you retire, you'll never work again.*

Welcome to the era of the "unretired." Millions of people are re-entering the workforce because of the rising cost of living, longer lifespans, and a desire for purpose and routine. It could mean consulting part-time, launching a small business, teaching, investing, or monetizing a lifelong hobby.

Modern retirement is about shifting into something sustainable, meaningful, and financially viable.

And no, it's not too late to plan. Even if you're playing catch-up, there's power in starting now. Increase your retirement contributions, streamline your expenses, and make intentional lifestyle choices that support your long-term goals. Every little bit helps.

It's also about protecting those you love. Retirement planning isn't just about beach vacations and bucket lists—it's also about estate planning. Work with professionals to set up wills, trusts, and powers of attorney. Make sure your assets are accounted for, your wishes are known, and your family isn't left guessing—or fighting—after you're gone.

One other thing—if you have a partner, get aligned. Retirement is a team sport. Talk through your vision. Agree on your goals. Make decisions together now so you don't face confusion or conflict later. Data shows that the lifespan of women is longer than men. It's vitally important for women to be empowered and engaged in all financial decisions.

Whatever the future holds for you and your family, you want to be able to manage your money with confidence, not with crisis and despair.

FINAL TRUTH: RETIREMENT ISN'T AN AGE—IT'S A NUMBER.

It's not about when you want to retire, it's about when you can retire—comfortably. That number looks different for everyone. What matters most is starting the plan today, so you have the freedom to choose tomorrow.

Because at the end of the day, retirement isn't about slowing down—it's about stepping fully into the life you've worked so hard to build.

It's about flying that plane you've always dreamed of. Setting sail for new adventures. Finally writing the book, launching the business, teaching at your alma mater, or pouring into the people and causes that light you up.

Because Money Movers don't "retire." We realign, reset, and rise.

Whether you're traveling the world, investing in your grandkids' futures, or mentoring the next generation of leaders—this season is yours to design. So, don't shrink your dreams to fit a traditional retirement model.

Expand your vision. You've earned it—and the best is still unfolding.

REFLECTION QUESTIONS:

- What does my ideal retirement look like?
- What steps can I take today to bring that vision closer?
- Am I financially prepared to protect my peace in this next chapter?

Bonus Chapter

Credit Check, Reality Check

Why Your Score Isn't Just a Number—it's a Power Move

Here's the deal: your credit score doesn't define your worth—but it absolutely influences your access.

Whether you're buying a car, applying for a mortgage, renting an apartment, or starting a business, that three-digit number is your financial reputation, and it can make or break your next move. And yet, a lot of people don't fully understand how it works—or how much power they actually have to shape it.

So, let's break it down.

CREDIT SCORE 101: WHAT IT REALLY MEANS

Think of your credit score like a financial GPA. It doesn't care how much you earn—it shows lenders how responsibly you handle what you borrow. Credit scores typically range between 300 and 850. The higher your score, the greater your access—to better loan terms, lower interest rates, and stronger negotiating power.

WHAT IMPACTS IT?

Most scoring models—like FICO—are based on five factors:

1. **Payment History (35%)** – Do you pay on time? This is the biggest factor. Even one missed payment can cause damage.
2. **Credit Utilization (30%)** – How much of your available credit are you using? Are you maxed out or managing wisely? Aim to stay below 30%, ideally under 10% if you want to flex.
3. **Credit Age (15%)** – Time builds trust. The longer your accounts stay open, the stronger your score.
4. **Credit Mix (10%)** – A variety of credit types (credit cards, loans, etc.) helps.
5. **New Credit (10%)** – Too many hard inquiries or new accounts in a short time can trigger a red flag and ding your score.

WHY IT MATTERS

A strong credit score is a silent superpower. It gives you:

- Lower interest rates = big savings over time
- Easier approvals for mortgages, rentals and major purchases
- Leverage in negotiating credit terms or refinancing
- Access to real estate, business capital and elite rewards cards
- Even lower insurance premiums and career opportunities (yes, some employers check)

On the flip side? A low score costs you—in money, time and peace of mind. But the good news? It's always fixable.

BOOST YOUR SCORE LIKE A PRO:

- **Pay on time—every time.** Automate it, calendar it, prioritize it.
- **Slash those balances.** If your credit cards are maxed out, focus on paying them down. High utilization is a deal-breaker.
- **Keep older accounts open.** Unless they're costing you fees, keep that history alive. Don't delete your proven track record.
- **Apply wisely and only when necessary.** Limit new applications. Too many inquiries do more harm than good.
- **Check your credit report.** You're entitled to a free report every year at annualcreditreport.com. Be sure to check all three bureaus and dispute any errors. They're more common than you think.

FINAL THOUGHT: CREDIT IS POWER-USE IT WISELY

Your credit score is more than a number—it's your financial passport. It either opens doors or keeps them closed.

LET'S BE REAL: IT'S EXPENSIVE TO BE POOR.

Bad credit doesn't just limit your options—it makes everything cost more. Higher interest rates. Bigger deposits. Denied approvals. Lost opportunities. When your financial foundation is shaky, even the basics become harder to access.

Knowledge is power—but action is how you build momentum.

Don't wait for a crisis—start now. Build your credit before you need it. Protect it like your future depends on it—because it does.

Because money moves—and those who move smart, move first.

Closing Chapter

From Surviving to Thriving

This Is Your Financial Power Move

If you've made it to this point in the book, take a moment and celebrate that. You showed up. You didn't just pick up a book. You opened your mind and picked up momentum. You chose to face your finances head-on—maybe in a way you never have before. You invested time, energy and courage into rewriting your money story—and that is no small feat.

Because the truth is, so many people don't even begin. They stay stuck in cycles of financial stress—not because they don't care—but because it feels too overwhelming. The fear of getting it wrong is paralyzing.

Now, this is your invitation to go further.

This isn't just a closing chapter. It's your opening act. You've learned that financial wellness is about building rhythm. It's about daily choices, intentional habits, and refusing to shrink in the face of challenges. You've shifted your mindset. You've explored your "why." You've seen what's possible when you take intentional action.

That's a *Money Move.*

And this is just the beginning.

Here's what to carry with you on your Money Moves journey:

- **Give yourself grace.** If you slip, recalibrate. Don't let one mistake erase all your progress.
- **Keep it simple.** Don't chase 15 goals at once. Focus on one bold step at a time and move with intention.
- **Break the silence.** Normalize money conversations. Start talking, start listening, start teaching, start transforming.
- **Invest in yourself.** Books, podcasts, workshops, coaching—whatever helps you grow, do it.
- **Believe in your ability to grow your wealth.** Because you can. You already are.

You didn't come this far to play small. You came to own your power, grow your wealth, and lead your life—with purpose, peace, and unapologetic clarity.

So, let's go. This is your next chapter—and you're the author. Every bold financial decision, every unapologetic boundary, every audacious dream you dare to fund.

Make the move. Then the next one. And keep going. You're built for this.

Ready for what's next? I've got you:

SUBSCRIBE TO THE *HER MONEY MOVES* PODCAST

Learn from women CEOs, entrepreneurs, and change-makers who've built wealth and success from the ground up. Real stories. Real strategies. Find us on YouTube @hermoneymovespodcast, Spotify, or at StaciLaToison.com.

JOIN THE MOVEMENT

Ready to turn ambition into action? Enroll in a Money Moves workshop. Book a private coaching session. Book me to speak at your next conference. Join our newsletter to gain tools, clarity, and confidence to build wealth, own your power, and upgrade your financial game. Visit www.stacilatoison.com, and step into your next level.

Dream Bigger!
Staci

Bonus Challenge

The 30-Day Financial Reset

Reclaim Your Cash.
Reinforce Your Power.

You've done the work. You've talked about your money, uncovered your money mindset, set bold goals, and faced the numbers head-on. Now it's time to activate all of it. Not "next month." Not "someday." Right now.

Let's make it fun. Let's gamify your progress.

This 30-day Financial Reset is about proving to yourself that even small, intentional choices can unlock big shifts. Money moves when you do. Let's go.

THE RULES ARE SIMPLE, THE IMPACT IS LASTING:

1. **Choose Your Financial Triggers**
   Pick 1–3 habits to pause for 30 days. Maybe it's Starbucks. DoorDash? Impulse buys? Streaming subscriptions? Identify the things that bleed money out of your wallet and press pause—on purpose.

2. **Track what you reclaim.**
   Every time you skip a spend, log the amount in a note, spreadsheet, or savings app. Transfer those dollars weekly to a "Power Fund." Don't just save—assign meaning to that money.

3. **Give your savings a purpose.**
   What's your why? Whether it's building an emergency cushion, crushing credit card debt, or stacking cash for a dream trip—name your goal and visualize it. Your "why" is your fuel. Let it drive every decision.

4. **Check in weekly.**
   Review what you've saved—and what you've learned. How do you feel? Are you surprised? Proud? Empowered? Noticing other habits you want to shift? That's the financial confidence you're building.

5. **Celebrate with Intention.**
   At the end of your 30 days, honor your progress—but make it meaningful. Treat yourself to dinner, go see a show you've been eyeing, or plan a self-care day that fuels your soul without draining your

wallet. You didn't just save money—you proved to yourself that you can pause, pivot, and move with purpose. That deserves celebration.

BONUS POWER PLAYS:

- Try a full "no-spend" weekend or weekday challenge and track the savings.
- Meal prep for the week—save money and reclaim your time.
- Unsubscribe from marketing emails or shopping apps that tempt you.
- Tuck your credit cards away to make spending less convenient.
- Invite a friend or partner to join you and turn it into an accountability challenge.

This isn't about perfection. It's about progress.

You don't have to overhaul your whole life overnight. But small, strategic moves build momentum—and momentum builds money.

This challenge is your reset. Your reminder. Your proof that you're not waiting on wealth—you're moving toward it.

Let this be your Money Move. Let this be your shift from spending on autopilot to saving with intention. Because financial freedom isn't a fantasy—it's a decision.

About the Author

Staci LaToison is an award-winning investor, podcaster, speaker, author, and consultant. She is the founder of Dream Big Ventures, a WBENC- and NMSDC-certified global consulting firm specializing in strategic planning, cost control, marketing, executive coaching, and keynote speaking.

With 22 years of global leadership at Chevron—managing billion-dollar budgets and teams across five continents, including expat assignments in China and Angola—she now partners with corporations and government agencies to drive innovative, high-impact solutions.

Staci is dedicated to elevating women in business. Through her *Her Money Moves* podcast and summits, she demystifies finance, empowering women to own their power, build wealth, and achieve financial independence. She invests in underrepresented startups, leads empowering workshops, and fosters a vibrant community dedicated to encouraging women and girls to dream bigger. She also leads impactful initiatives through her nonprofit, the Dreamgirls Foundation, mobilizing women and youth through entrepreneurship, financial literacy, and community-building efforts.

A fierce advocate for diabetes care, Staci is a proud Type 1 Diabetes Mom and is actively involved with Breakthrough T1D. Her dream is to one day help find a cure, and she works passionately to raise awareness and support for families navigating life with T1D.

Staci was honored with *Staci LaToison Day* in Houston and *Her Money Moves Day* in Harris County. A co-author of *Latinas in VC and Fortaleza, she was named 2025 Woman of Distinction and Global Business Innovation Icon.* Recognized among *Houston's Top 30 Influential Women* and *Latino Leaders Most Influential Latinas* (2024, 2025), she also received the *Mendoza Ventures Funder of the Year, L'ATTITUDE Ventures Game Changer Award, Chase Latina Executive Achievement Award, and Houston Business Journal Women Who Mean Business in Energy Award.*

A proud Puerto Rican and Cuban single mother of two, Staci has been featured in Forbes and Nasdaq and was selected for Finland's 90 Day Finn Program and the USGLC Next Gen Global Leaders Network. She serves on the University of Houston, Angeles Investors, Houston Hospice, and Discovery Green Conservancy boards and is a member of the Latino Corporate Directors Association and Women Presidents Organization.

Made in United States
North Haven, CT
11 November 2026

22097464R00046